CURVES AHEAD!

No-Fear
Techniques—
Spectacular Quilts

Susan Nelsen
Loraine Manwaring

Dedication

We dedicate this book to our children—for all the curves they've thrown us. You've added interest to life beyond our wildest dreams. Thanks, Michael, Erik, Jonathan, Tyler, Daniel, Kristin, Becky, Kyle, and Emily!

Acknowledgements

We want to thank:

Our families for always being such good sports as you've endured the frenzy of our sewing, quilting, and writing for all our books;

Pamela Mostek and All American Crafts for their confidence in us to write this book;

Oliso for providing us with the ultimate in steam irons.

Published by

All American Crafts, Inc.
7 Waterloo Road
Stanhope, NJ 07874
www.allamericancrafts.com

Publisher | **Jerry Cohen**

Chief Executive Officer | **Darren Cohen**

Product Development
Director | **Brett Cohen**

Editor | **Sue Harvey**

Art Director | **Kelly Albertson**

Photography | **Van Zandbergen Photography**

Illustrations | **Roni Palmisano**

Product Development
Manager | **Pamela Mostek**

Vice President/Quilting Advertising
& Marketing | **Carol Newman**

Printed in China
ISBN: 978-0-9819762-8-0
Library of Congress Control
Number: 2011927126

www.allamericancrafts.com

Curves Ahead!
Don't Shy Away

Curves Ahead! is not a warning sign when it comes to quilts. Instead, with our No-Fear approach to curves, it's actually an invitation to speed right into the curves that give your quilts that extra pedal-to-the-metal punch.

Maybe you've shied away from making a quilt with curved seams. In the past we've done the same because those curved seams looked just a little too tricky to navigate. Those days are behind us now. We decided to put ourselves in the driver's seat when it came to curves and face them head on! No more intimidation. We developed No-Fear Curves and never looked in the rearview mirror!

In this book we'll share our tips and tricks to drive away all your fears of sewing curves. Using our Tame a C-Curve method, you'll sew a perfectly smooth curve in a traditional Drunkard's Path. Strip piecing takes on a new look when you use our Steer Into an S-Curve technique. Your quilts will go from nice to WOW with a curvy outer edge. Try our Round a Base Line and Fast S-Curve Finish.

With a few simple supplies, tools, and our tips, you'll be cruising your way through all the projects as you travel through this book. Our freehand curves are as fun and liberating as the open road so let your imagination run wild with the possibilities. In fact, we predict you'll become veteran curve navigators before you know it! But don't stop with the quilts you find in the book. With your No-Fear Curves confidence, you'll be ready to add curves to other quilts too.

Curves Ahead!—are you ready for a whirlwind spin around the block? We have the map, so hop in and enjoy the ride as you learn to navigate No-Fear Curves. Start your engines … get ready, get set, go! Join us on our road trip of fabulous curvy seams.

—Loraine and Susan

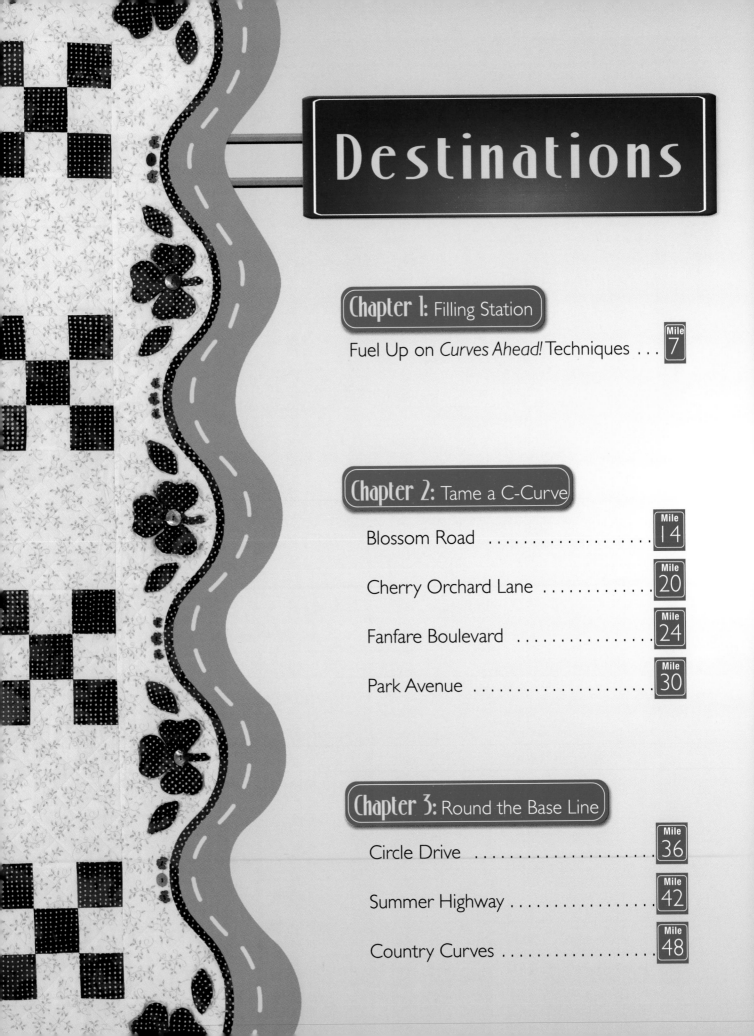

Destinations

Chapter 1

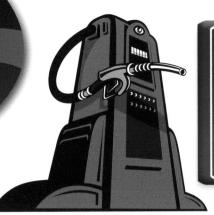

Filling Station: Fill Up on Curves Ahead! Techniques

Every car needs fuel, so fill up with our special techniques to make the engines roar and the curves flow! Get ready, get set, go!

TAME A C-CURVE

Use this method for curved seams in traditional blocks that have pieces cut with templates, such as the Drunkard's Path and Dogwood blocks. This method is foolproof, tucks are non-existent, and pins are not required.

Materials needed:
- Water-soluble marker
- ¼" double-sided transparent, water-soluble tape, such as WashAway Wonder Tape by Collins or Dritz WashAway Wonder Tape

1. Using a water-soluble marker, mark the fabric with any dots indicated on the project templates as shown. Mark the dots so they can be seen from the front and the back of the block pieces.

2. Cut a piece of tape just slightly longer than the length of the convex curved edge of the pie-shaped piece. Apply the tape to the right side along the curved edge. The edge of the piece will curl as the tape is applied. Press the tape firmly in place with your fingers. Remove the paper backing from the tape.

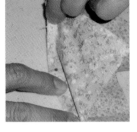

3. Align the dots and the ends of the 2 fabric pieces, right sides together, and finger-press in place. Then gently pull on the curves of both pieces, matching the curved edges, and finger-press in place. There should be no puckers.

4. Sew a ¼" seam and press the seam allowance following the instructions in your project—a *perfect* curve!

ROUND THE BASE LINE

Use this method to create a scalloped outside edge, adding a spectacular one of a kind touch to your quilt!

Materials needed:
- Freezer paper
- Water-soluble marker

1. Trim the batting and backing even with the top. (Refer to The Finish Line on page 75 for more information.)

2. If your quilt is square, cut 4 strips of freezer paper the length of the quilt center by the width of the border.

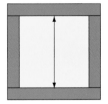

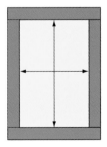

3. If your quilt is a rectangle, cut 2 strips of freezer paper the length of the quilt center by the width of the border. Cut 2 strips the width of the quilt center by the width of the border.

4. To make 3 scallops on each side (see Country Curves on page 48), fold each strip in half and in half again to make 4 layers as shown. Mark a gentle curve with a pencil on the top layer. When you are satisfied with your marked curve, cut along the marked line and unfold as shown

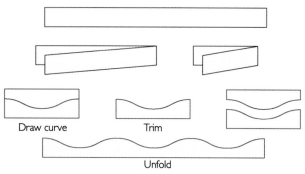

Draw curve   Trim

Unfold

5. To make more than 3 scallops on each side (see Cherry Orchard Lane on page 20), fold the strip as directed in step 4, then fold the layered strip in half to crease the center. Unfold. Fold the folded end in to meet the creased centerline as shown. Draw a gentle curve on the top layer. Cut along the marked line and unfold.

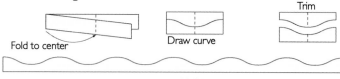

Fold to center   Draw curve   Trim

Unfold

6. Center the freezer-paper cutouts, with shiny side down, along the respective sides of your quilt as shown and press in place. Use a water-soluble marker to mark the curved edges of your quilt. To round the corners of the quilt, line up the curved edge of a plate or circle template between the ends of the freezer-paper strips as shown, overlapping as necessary to make a smooth corner curve. Carefully remove the freezer paper, and cut along the curved edges of your quilt. The quilt is now ready to add the binding.

7. If your quilt is a rectangle and you want more scallops on the longer sides than on the shorter sides, cut 4 curved pieces of freezer paper the length of the shorter sides. Fold and draw a scallop as in step 2. Then cut 2 of the pieces exactly in half along the center fold. Place both ends on the border of the quilt as directed in step 3. This will leave a gap in the middle of each long side. You decide if you need another curve or two added. Make another copy of

the drawn curve (or curves). Center this on the side where you are adding the curves and draw connecting lines to smooth out the curves. Both sides will be balanced, but not duplicates of the shorter sides. The scallops may not all be exactly the same, but it's fine.

STEER INTO AN S-CURVE
Use these simple techniques to cut and stitch freehand curves—no marking, no measuring, no pins, no templates—No Fear!

SINGLE S-CURVE
We've used this freehand technique where we traditionally would have a straight seam, such as along a border or in a Rail Fence block.

If you are adapting a pattern and incorporating a curved seam instead of a straight seam, you'll need to cut your fabric strips wider and longer to accommodate the addition of the curve. You'll have to do some experimenting for the pattern that you want to adapt. To give you some idea, here's an example from our experience: *Traditional straight seam*—With a ¼" seam, two 3" strips seamed together produce one 5"-wide finished section. *Curved seam*—Two 3" strips seamed together with this curved seam technique will create a 3½"-wide finished section.

Materials needed:

- 2 fabric strips, cut the dimensions needed for your project
- 1"-wide blue painter's tape
- Fine-tip marker

1. Place the first strip right side up on the cutting mat. Place the second fabric strip right side up, overlapping the edges to be sewn by 1" as shown.

2. Place a piece of painter's tape over the 1" overlapped area of the fabrics, securing the ends of the tape to the mat. Press the tape lightly onto the fabric. The tape defines the cutting area and stabilizes the fabrics for cutting.

3. Within the area of the tape, use a rotary cutter to cut gentle curves along the length of the layered strips, working from edge to edge on the tape. The more gentle the curve, the easier it will be to sew the curve. Starting and stopping the cut with a straight line will help you in sewing the seam.

4. To the left of the cut, gently lift the tape (still attached to fabric 2 strip) and discard. Gently remove the remaining tape. Move fabric strip 2 away from strip 1, exposing a small cut strip of fabric strip 1. Discard this small strip as well.

5. Turn both fabrics 1 and 2 face down on the mat and slide the curves to fit perfectly together.

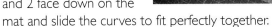

With the marker, mark the hills and valleys of the curves with a tick mark on the edge of each fabric.

6. At the sewing machine with right sides together and fabric strip 2 on top of fabric strip 1, hold the starting edges of the strips even. Take five or six stitches, sewing a ¼" seam, and stop stitching with the needle in the down position. Align the first set of tick marks and sew toward the tick marks. As you sew the seam, keep the bottom fabric flat on the machine and gently maneuver the top strip to keep the edges of both strips even. Sew from one set of tick marks to the next, aligning the edges as you go. Complete the seam.

7. Press the seam from the right side using the tip of the iron to open the strips. Press the entire seam from the right side before turning it over to check that the entire seam is pressed in the same direction. You can repeat these steps to add additional strips, depending on your project. Square up the ends of the strip and cut the strip section into the required size for your project. *Perfect* curves!

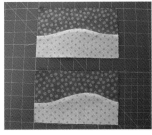

DOUBLE S-CURVE
Using two fabric colors, this method creates a curving river of one color within the second color of fabric. These curved seams require wider strips than you might expect. If you are adapting your own pattern, you will have to experiment to determine necessary strip widths. To help you though, here's an example from our experience: Two 3" strips, following this curved-seam technique, will produce a 3"-wide finished section.

Materials needed:
- 2 fabric strips, cut the dimensions needed for your project
- 1"-wide blue painter's tape
- Fine-tip marker

1. Place strip 1 right side up on the cutting mat and place strip 2 right side up centered on top of strip 1. Place a piece of painter's tape down the center of the strips as shown. (Your project may have strips of two different widths, so center the narrower strip on top of the wider strip, right sides up.)

2. Within the area of the tape, use a rotary cutter to cut gentle curves from edge to edge on the tape, cutting along the length of the strips. The more gentle the curve, the easier it will be to sew the curve. Starting and stopping the cut with a straight line will help you in sewing the seam.

3. Gently remove the tape. Lift the top piece to the left of the cut and place it face down on the left side of the mat. Lift the top piece to the right of the cut and place it face down on the right side of the mat.

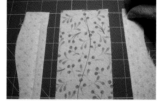

4. Lift the bottom piece to the right of the cut and place it face down to match to the strip on the left edge of the mat. Lift the bottom piece to the left of the cut and place it face down to match to the strip on the right edge of the mat as shown. You have 2 sections with curves that fit together perfectly.

5. On the wrong side of the fabric, mark the hills and valleys of the curves on the edges of each strip set with a small tick mark as shown.

6. With right sides together, hold the starting edges of the strips even. Take five or six stitches, sewing a ¼" seam and stop stitching with the needle in the down position. Align the first set of tick marks and sew toward the tick marks. As you sew the seam, keep the bottom fabric flat on the machine and gently maneuver the top strip to keep the edges of both strips even. Sew from one set of tick marks to the next, aligning the edges as you go. Complete the seam. Repeat for the second set of strips.

7. Press the seams from the right side using the tip of the iron to open the strips. Press each seam from the right side before turning it over to check that the entire seam is pressed in the same direction.

8. Decide which strip color you want to be the center curve of the completed unit. Place the two pieced strips right sides together, aligning the edges of the center-color strips. Use a rotary cutter to make a straight cut on the center-color edges. Sew the sections together along these edges, using a ¼" seam, and press the strip open.

9. Cut this section the width indicated in your project instructions, keeping the straight seam centered along the length of the strip. Now the section can be cut into the size called for in your project. *Perfect* curves!

FAST S-CURVE FINISH
Try this freewheeling method for freehand border curves. It is fast and easy to do.

Materials needed:
• 1"-wide blue painter's tape

1. Place blue tape along the edge of the quilt. If you want to cut the corners shown for this quilt, measure about the same distance from each corner for the correct tape placement.

2. With a rotary cutter, cut a gentle curve within the area of the tape. As you come to corners, continue a curve around the corner.

MAKING YO-YOS

1. Cut a circle template twice the diameter plus ½" of the finished yo-yo. Trace the template onto the yo-yo fabric and cut out the circle.

2. Fold under a scant ¼" along the edge of the circle and stitch along the fold of the fabric, using a running stitch. (We use hand-quilting thread because it's extra strong, and it will secure the yo-yo.) As you start to stitch, leave a tail of thread about 3"-long. Go completely around the circle without backstitching. Don't cut your thread yet.

3. Now pull the thread tail and needle thread to gather up the fabric circle. Secure the gathers with two or three stitches and a knot. The edges will gather to the center, and you will have a small opening in the center of the yo-yo. Take three or four stitches to secure the gathers, knot and trim your thread. Now flatten the yo-yo with the opening centered in the front. You can control the size of the opening with the size of your gathering stitches: the larger the running stitch, the smaller the opening in the center.

Chapter 2

Tame a C-Curve

Blossom Road

← **This Exit**

Nice and easy driving ahead when you use the Tame a C-Curve technique to create this fun, flower quilt made from bright polka dots and busy prints. The posies really pop with the vintage style yo-yos in the center. Definitely a winner at the finish line!

Finished Quilt: 35" × 35"
Finished Block: 10" × 10"

What You'll Need

All yardages are based on 42"-wide fabric.

✧ ¾ yard of black-on-white print for the blocks

✧ ¾ yard of white-on-black print for the blocks

✧ ¾ yard of black-with-white dot for the border and the yo-yos

✧ ½ yard of white-with-black dot for the binding

✧ 9 fat eighths of a variety of polka-dot fabrics for the flowers

✧ 41" × 41" piece of backing fabric

✧ 41" × 41" piece of batting

✧ Template plastic

✧ Water-soluble marker

✧ 13 yards of ¼" double-sided transparent, water-soluble tape

CUTTING IT UP

– *All measurements include ¼"-wide seam allowances.*

– *Templates A, B, and C for this project are on page 77. Copy the templates at 100% and trace onto template plastic. Cut out the templates and mark the dots as indicated on each template. Use a water-soluble marker to mark the A pieces on the fabric front and the B pieces on the fabric back.*

From the black-on-white print, cut:

✧ 36 pieces, using template B front side up

From the white-on-black print, cut:

✧ 36 pieces, using template B back side up

From the black-with-white dot, cut:

✧ 4 strips 2½" × 42"

✧ 9 pieces, using template C

From the white-with-black dot, cut:

✧ 4 strips 2½" × 42" (for binding)

From each of the assorted polka dot fabrics, cut:

✧ 4 pieces, using template A

MAKING THE BLOCKS

1. Refer to Tame a C-Curve on page 7 and follow the directions to sew the curve for the Dogwood block. Sew one A piece between a white B piece (on the left) and a black B piece (on the right), matching the dots. Press the seam toward the B pieces. *Note: be sure that the fabric placement is the same for each unit.* Repeat to make a total of 36 units, using all the A and B pieces.

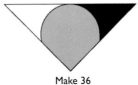

Make 36

2. Join 2 matching color units from step 1 as shown. Press the seams in the direction of the arrow. Repeat to sew all the units from step 1 into pairs.

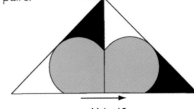

Make 18

3. Join 2 matching units from step 2 as shown. Before pressing, remove the vertical center stitches in the seam allowances on both sides of each unit; then press the seam allowances in opposite directions. Where the 4 points meet in the middle, press the seams open so the seams make a tiny square. This eliminates extra bulk when pressing. Complete 9 flower blocks.

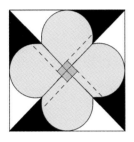 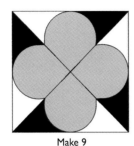

Make 9

PUTTING IT TOGETHER

1. Arrange the blocks in 3 horizontal rows as shown. Sew the blocks in each row together, pressing the seam allowances in opposite directions from row to row. Join the rows. Press the seams in one direction.

2. Refer to Borders on page 75 and use the black-with-white dot 2½" strips for the border.

FINISHING IT UP

Refer to The Finish Line on page 75 for details regarding each of these steps.

1. Layer the quilt top with the batting and the backing; then baste, unless you plan to take your quilt to a longarm quilter.

2. Hand- or machine-quilt as desired. The many polka dots in this quilt just really keep the eyes busy, so an elaborate quilting design or use

Quilt Layout

of special thread would just get lost. I decided to quilt this with a tight, loopy meandering pattern, using white thread. The result was the addition of texture and softness—very pleasing!

3. Use the white-with-black dot 2½" strips to bind the quilt edges.

4. Refer to Making Yo-Yos on page 11 to make 9 yo-yos, using the black-with-white dot C pieces. Hand-sew them to the flower centers.

5. Sew a hanging sleeve to the back of the quilt if desired.

BLOSSOM ROAD, 35" x 35", by Loraine Manwaring

Dogwood Trail

A SECOND CURVE OF COLOR

Same road map, same curves—entirely different results! If you keep your eyes on the curves long enough, the shades of soft pink and jade glass green seem to pop and fade differently. Don't shy away…these No-Fear curves are easy and create a fabulous look to the quilt.

DOGWOOD TRAIL, 46" x 56", by Loraine Manwaring

Cherry Orchard Lane

← This Exit

Relax and enjoy the curves on Cherry Orchard Lane using our fearless approach to piecing curves. We've combined a traditional Drunkard's Path Block with our Tame a C-Curve technique to create an updated curvy version that may look tough to navigate but is easy-to-do with your new-found curves confidence.

Finished Quilt: 70" × 94"
Finished Block: 12" × 12"

What You'll Need

All yardages are based on 42"-wide fabric.

✧ 4½ yards of red check for the blocks and the bias binding

✧ 3½ yards of yellow print for the blocks

✧ 1¼ yards of green print for the border

✧ 78" × 102" piece of backing fabric

✧ 78" × 102" piece of batting

✧ 48 buttons of assorted sizes

✧ Template plastic

✧ Freezer paper

✧ Water-soluble marker

✧ 8½ yards ¼" double-sided transparent, water-soluble tape

CUTTING IT UP

– *All measurements include ¼"-wide seam allowances.*

– *Templates A and B are on page 79. Copy the templates at 100% and trace onto template plastic. Cut out the templates and mark the dots as indicated on each template.*

From the red check, cut:

✧ 6 strips 12½"× 42"; cut into 18 squares 12½" × 12½"

✧ 9 strips 4½" × 42"; cut into 68 pieces, using template A

✧ 1 square 33" × 33" (for binding)

From the yellow print, cut:

✧ 6 strips 12½" × 42"; cut into 17 squares 12½" × 12½"

✧ 9 strips 4½" × 42"; cut into 72 pieces, using template A

From the green print, cut:

✧ 8 strips 5" × 42"

MAKING THE BLOCKS

1. Mark the corners of *all* of the 12½" × 12½" squares using template B. Cut along the marked lines. Discard the pie pieces that you cut. Using a water-soluble pen, mark the center dot on the right side of the fabric on each corner curve as shown.

Make 18   Make 17

2. To complete the Drunkard's Path blocks, refer to Tame a C-Curve on page 7. Press the seams toward the corners. Make 17 yellow blocks and 18 red blocks as shown.

Make 17   Make 18

PUTTING IT TOGETHER

1. Arrange the blocks in 7 horizontal rows as shown, alternating the position of the red and yellow blocks from row to row as shown. Sew the blocks in each row together, pressing the seam allowances in opposite directions from row to row. Join the rows. Press the seam allowances in one direction.

2. Refer to Borders on page 75 and use the green print 5" strips for the border.

FINISHING IT UP

Refer to The Finish Line on page 75 for details regarding each of the following steps.

1. Layer the quilt top with the batting and the backing; then baste, unless you plan to take your quilt to a long-arm quilter.

2. Hand- or machine-quilt as desired. I machine-quilted medallions in the center of each block and a large meandering design in the remaining areas. I added a scalloped pattern over many of the seam lines to pull the quilting designs together.

3. Refer to Round the Baseline on page XX to cut the scalloped border.

4. Refer to Bias-Cut Binding on page 76 to make 400" of continuous bias binding from the red check 33" square or use your favorite method to make bias binding. Use this bias binding to complete the quilt.

5. Attach the buttons as shown in the photograph of the quilt.

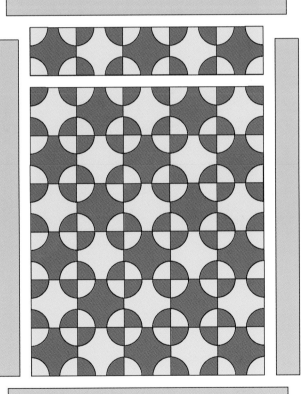

Quilt Layout

CHERRY ORCHARD LANE, 70" x 94", by Loraine Manwaring

There are curves ahead on Fanfare Boulevard, but you'll take them with ease with your new fearless techniques for curves. The background print of elegant fans and the striking colors in the medallion center will make this quilt a favorite stop on your quilting road trip.

Finished Quilt: 67" × 67"

Finished Block: 7" × 7"

What You'll Need

All yardages are based on 42"-wide fabric.

✧ 2½ yards of black print for the blocks and border

✧ 1¾ yards of yellow tone-on-tone for the blocks, border, and binding

✧ 1 yard of green tone-on-tone for the blocks

✧ ¾ yard of pink tone-on-tone for the blocks

✧ 75" × 75" piece of backing fabric

✧ 75" × 75" piece of batting

✧ Template plastic

✧ Water-soluble marker

✧ 18 yards of ¼" double-sided transparent, water-soluble tape

CUTTING IT UP

– All measurements include ¼"-wide seam allowances.

– Templates A and B for this project are on page 78. Copy the templates at 100% and trace onto template plastic. Cut out the templates and mark the dots as indicated on each template. Cut the B pieces as shown.

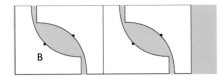

From the black print, cut:

✧ 7 strips 7½" × 42"; cut into 44 pieces, using template B

✧ 7 strips 3½" × 42"

From the yellow tone-on-tone, cut:

✧ 4 strips 5¾" × 42"; cut into 32 pieces, using template A

✧ 13 strips 2½" × 42" (border and binding)

From the green tone-on-tone , cut:

✧ 3 strips 7½" × 42"; cut into 20 pieces, using template B

✧ 1 strip 5¾" × 42"; cut into 4 pieces, using template A

From the pink tone-on-tone, cut:

✧ 4 strips 5¾" × 42"; cut into 28 pieces, using template A

MAKING THE BLOCKS

1. Refer to Tame a C-Curve on page 7 and follow the directions to make the Drunkard's Path block. Using all the A and B pieces, make the various color combinations as shown.

Make 16

Make 24

Make 4

Make 12

Make 8

PUTTING IT TOGETHER

1. Refer to the quilt layout and arrange Drunkard's Path blocks, turning the blocks as shown. Sew each row and press the seam allowances in opposite directions from row to row. Then join the rows together and press to make the quilt center.

2. Referring to Borders on page 75, use 6 of the yellow 2½" strips for the inside border and use the black 3½" strips for the outside border.

FINISHING IT UP

Refer to The Finish Line on page 75 for details regarding each of these steps.

1. Layer the quilt top, batting, and backing; then baste, unless you plan to take your quilt to a long-arm quilter.

2. Hand- or machine-quilt as desired. I machine-quilted this with black thread so the quilting would stand out in the light colored areas, adding texture to the quilt.

3. Use the remaining yellow 2½" strips to bind the edges of the quilt.

Quilt Layout

FANFARE BOULEVARD, 67" x 67", by Susan Nelsen

Road Race

SECOND CURVE OF COLOR

You're on the curvy road to the finish line in this dramatically different version that uses racing flag colors of red, black, and white to create this WOW winning quilt. No worries about the curves—take them head on and the results will be fabulous. Freehand-cut curves on the outside edge add a fun touch at the finish line.

ROAD RACE, 67" x 67", by Susan Nelsen

Park Avenue

← This Exit

Uptown fabrics and a No-Fear approach to the curves along the way will put you on the road to Park Avenue. The curved block may look intimidating, but don't shy away. It's just one curved patch done in different fabric combinations. You'll be first across the finish line with this dramatic quilt.

Finished Quilt: 59" × 75"
Finished Block: 16" × 16"

What You'll Need

All yardages are based on 42" fabric.

✧ 2¼ yards of dark blue print for the blocks and binding

✧ 1½ yards of dark abstract print for the blocks and inside border

✧ 1¼ yards of tan floral for the blocks and outside border

✧ 1 yard of red print for the blocks

✧ 1 yard of olive print for the blocks

✧ ½ yard of blue floral for the blocks

✧ 67" × 83" piece of backing fabric

✧ 67" × 83" piece of batting

✧ Template plastic

✧ Water-soluble marker

✧ 23 yards of ¼" double-sided transparent, water-soluble tape

CUTTING IT UP

— All measurements include ¼"-wide seam allowances.

— Templates A and B for this project are on page 79. Copy the templates at 100% and trace onto template plastic. Cut out the templates and mark the dots as indicated on each template.

From the dark blue print, cut:

✧ 10 strips 4½" × 42"; cut into 96 pieces, using template B

✧ 7 strips 2½" × 42" (for binding)

From the dark abstract print, cut:

✧ 5 strips 4½" × 42"; cut into 48 pieces, using template A

✧ 6 strips 2½" × 42"

From the tan floral, cut:

✧ 7 strips 3½" × 42"

✧ 4 strips 3⅛" × 42"; cut into 48 pieces, using template A

From the red print, cut:

✧ 8 strips 3⅛" × 42"; cut into 96 pieces, using template B

From the olive print, cut:

✧ 5 strips 4½" × 42"; cut into 48 pieces, using template B

From the blue floral fabric, cut:

✧ 4 strips 3⅛" × 42"; cut into 48 pieces, using template A

MAKING THE BLOCKS

Refer to Tame a C-Curve on page 7 and follow the directions to make the Drunkard's Path block.

1. Using all the A and B pieces, make the various color combinations as shown.

Make 96   Make 48   Make 48

2. Arranging units from step 1, make 12 blocks as shown.

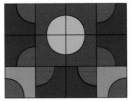
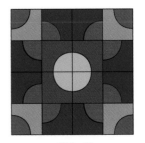

Make 12

PUTTING IT TOGETHER

1. Arrange the blocks in 4 horizontal rows as shown. Sew the blocks in each row together, pressing the seams in opposite directions from row to row. Join the rows. Press the seams in one direction.

2. Refer to Borders on page 75, use the dark abstract print 2½" strips for the inside border. Repeat to use the tan floral 3½" strips for the outside border.

FINISHING IT UP

Refer to The Finish Line on page 75 for specific instructions regarding each of the following steps.

1. Layer the quilt top with the batting and the backing; baste, unless you plan to take your quilt to a long-arm quilter.

2. Hand- or machine-quilt as desired. Since this block pattern, as well as the fabric used in this quilt, is so "busy," I didn't think elaborate machine quilting was necessary. I simply quilted a rather large stipple over the entire quilt, and the results were very pleasing.

3. Use the dark blue print 2½" strips to bind the quilt edges.

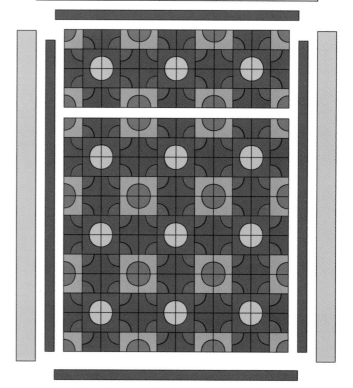

Quilt Layout

PARK AVENUE,
50" x 70",
by Loraine Manwaring

Chapter 3

Round the Base Line

Circle Drive

← This Exit

Traveling along on your quilting road trip, you may think you see Curves Ahead, but then you realize it's just the illusion of curves. This quilt is just the same. Its straight seams give the elegant look of curves, but you won't have to slow down to navigate them. In fact, you won't even have to use your No-Fear approach to curves—it will just look like you did!

Finished Quilt: 78" × 78"
Finished Block: 9" × 9"

What You'll Need

All yardages are based on 42"-wide fabric.

✧ 2½ yards of blue print for the Nine-Patch blocks and outside border
✧ 2½ yards of dark blue print for the Nine-Patch blocks and bias binding
✧ 1⅔ yards of light blue print for the Circle blocks
✧ ¾ yard of brown mottled for the Circle blocks
✧ ¾ yard of stripe for the inside border
✧ ½ yard of black/brown print for the Circle blocks
✧ 86" × 86" piece of backing fabric
✧ 86" × 86" piece of batting
✧ Freezer paper
✧ Water-soluble marker

CUTTING IT UP
– *All measurements include ¼"-wide seam allowances.*

From the blue print, cut:
✧ 11 strips 3½" × 42"
✧ 8 strips 5½" × 42"

From the dark blue print, cut:
✧ 13 strips 3½" × 42"
✧ 1 square 30" × 30" (for binding)

From the light blue print, cut:
✧ 5 strips 3⅞" × 42"; cut into 48 squares 3⅞" × 3⅞"; cut once diagonally to yield 96 triangles
✧ 4 strips 3½" × 42"; cut into 48 squares 3½" × 3½"
✧ 4 strips 3½" × 42"

From the brown mottled, cut:
✧ 5 strips 3⅞" × 42"; cut into 48 squares 3⅞" × 3⅞"; cut once diagonally to yield 96 triangles

From the stripe, cut:
✧ 7 strips 2½" × 42"

From the black/brown print, cut:
✧ 2 strips 3½" × 42"

MAKING THE BLOCKS
You'll make 2 types of blocks, the Circle block and the Nine-Patch block.

Circle Blocks

1. To make the Circle block, with right sides together, sew a light blue triangle to a brown triangle as shown to make a triangle-square unit. Press the seam allowance toward the brown. Trim off the extended dog ears. Repeat to make a total of 96 half-square triangles, using all the light blue and brown triangles.

Make 96

2. Sew a light blue 3½" square between 2 triangle-square units from step 1 as shown. Press the seam allowances toward the blue square. Repeat to make a total of 48.

Make 48

3. Sew a black/brown 3½" × 42" strip between 2 light blue 3½" × 42" strips as shown. Press the seam allowances toward the light blue. Make 2 strip sets. Then cut twenty-four 3½" sections.

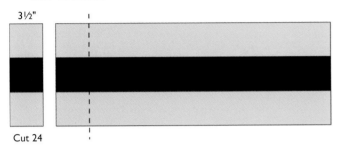

3½"

Cut 24

4. Sew a section from step 3 between 2 sections from step 2 to complete a Circle block. Press the seam allowances toward the center section. Complete a total of 24 blocks.

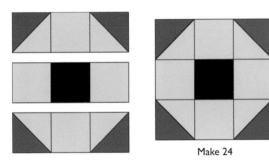

Make 24

Nine-Patch Blocks

1. Sew a blue 3½" × 42" strip between 2 dark blue 3½" × 42" strips. Press seam allowances toward the dark blue. Make a total of 5 strip sets. Then cut fifty 3½" sections.

3½"

Cut 50

2. Sew a dark blue strip between 2 blue strips as shown. Press the seam allowances toward the brown. Make a total of 3 strip sets. Then cut twenty-five 3½" sections.

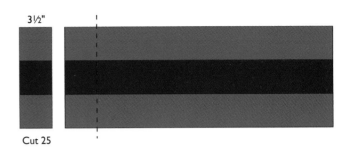

3½"

Cut 25

3. Arrange a section from step 2 between 2 sections from step 1 as shown to complete a Nine-Patch block. Press the seam allowances away from the center row. Repeat to make a total of 25 blocks.

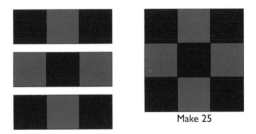

Make 25

PUTTING IT TOGETHER

1. Arrange the blocks into 7 horizontal rows as shown, alternating the position of the Circle and Nine-Patch blocks in each row and from row to row as shown. Sew the blocks in each row together, pressing the seam allowances toward the Nine-Patch blocks. Join the rows. Press the seam allowances in one direction.

2. Referring to Borders on page 75, use the 2½" stripe strips for the inside border and the 5½" blue print strips for the outside border.

FINISHING IT UP

Refer to The Finish Line on page 75 for details regarding each of these steps.

1. Layer the quilt top with the batting and the backing; baste, unless you plan to take your quilt to a longarm quilter.

2. Hand- or machine-quilt as desired. Since the quilt blocks in this quilt definitely suggest circles and motion and the edges are full of curves, machine quilting it with the curves and motion of large, over-all stippling seemed just right.

3. Refer to Round the Baseline on page 7 to cut the outside scalloped edge of your quilt.

4. Refer to Bias-Cut Binding on page 76 to make 330" of continuous bias binding from the dark blue print 30" square or use your favorite method to make bias binding. Use this bias binding to complete the quilt.

Quilt Layout

CIRCLE DRIVE, 78" x 78", by Loraine Manwaring

Summer Highway

← This Exit

The curves are easy and the warm summer sun is shining down as you travel along the quilting highway. With your No-Fear approach to curves, you can sit back and enjoy the ride as you create this curvy quilt with ease. Delicious ice-cream colors and unexpected curves in the borders combine to create a delightful summertime look.

Finished Quilt: 66" x 73"
Finished Blocks: 3½" x 3½" and 8½" x 8½"

What You'll Need

All yardages are based on 42"-wide fabric.

✧ 1½ yards of brown floral for the center

✧ 1¼ yards of pink print for the inside border and corner blocks

✧ 1 yard of brown polka dot for the outside border

✧ 1 yard of brown diagonal stripe for the outside border

✧ ¾ yard of brown mottled for the half-circles and corner blocks

✧ 1 yard brown print for bias binding

✧ 74" x 81" piece of backing fabric

✧ 74" x 81" piece of batting

✧ Template plastic

✧ 56 buttons—an assortment of colors and sizes for the embellishments

CUTTING IT UP

– *All measurements include ¼"-wide seam allowances.*

– *The circle template is on page 77. Copy the template at 100% and trace onto template plastic. Cut out the template and add markings as indicated on the template.*

From the brown floral, cut:

✧ 1 rectangle 39" x 46"

From the pink print, cut:

✧ 6 strips 4" x 42"; cut into 4 squares 4" x 4" and 96 pieces 2¼" x 4"

✧ 3 strips 2¾" x 42"; cut into 8 pieces 2¾" x 9" and 8 pieces 2¾" x 4½"

✧ 1 strip 1¾" x 42"; cut into 16 squares 1¾" x 1¾"

From the brown polka dot, cut:

✧ 3 strips 10½" x 42"; cut into 30 pieces 4" x 10½"

From the brown diagonal stripe, cut:

✧ 3 strips 9" x 42"; cut into 26 pieces 4" x 9"

From the brown mottled, cut:

✧ 1 strip 4½" x 42"; cut into 4 squares 4½" x 4½"

✧ 5 strips 3½" x 42"; cut into 48 circles, using the circle template

From the brown print, cut:

✧ 1 square 30" x 30" (for binding)

MAKING THE BLOCKS

You'll be making blocks for the inside border and blocks for the quilt corners.

Inside Border Blocks

1. Place 2 brown circles right sides together. Sew a ¼" seam completely around the outside edge of the circles. Repeat to complete 24.

Make 24

2. Cut each circle in half as shown and turn the half-circles right side out. Press the curved edge of the half-circle. Repeat this for all the sewn circles. You'll have 48 half-circles.

Make 48

3. Sew a half-circle between 2 pink 2¼" x 4" pieces, centering the half-circle in the seam as shown. Press the seam away from the half-circle. Complete 48 blocks for the inside border.

Make 48

Corner Blocks

1. Using a soft-lead pencil and a see-through ruler, draw a diagonal line from corner to corner on the back of each pink 1¾" square.

2. With right sides together, place a 1¾" square on each corner of a brown 4½" square as shown. Stitch on the drawn line. Trim the seams to ¼" and press the triangles toward the corners. Repeat to complete 4 snowballs.

Make 4

3. Sew a pink 2¾" x 4½" piece to opposite sides of a snowball and press. Then sew a pink 2¾" x 9" piece to the top and bottom of the block and press. Make 4 corner blocks.

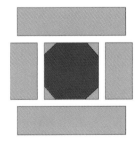

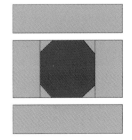 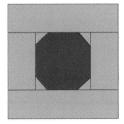

Make 4

PUTTING IT TOGETHER

1. Refer to the quilt layout and arrange the blocks for the inside border around the quilt center. Note the orientation of the half-circles in each row. Sew 13 blocks together for each side row and press. Sew the side rows to the center and press toward the center.

2. Sew 11 blocks together for the top and bottom rows and press. Sew a pink 4" square to the ends of each row. Add the rows to the quilt center. Press the seams toward the center.

3. For the side rows of the outside border, sew 7 stripe pieces between 8 polka-dot pieces as shown in the quilt layout and press the seams toward the shorter stripe pieces. Join those to the quilt center.

4. For the top and bottom rows of the outside border, sew 6 stripe pieces between 7 polka-dot pieces as shown and press the seams toward the shorter stripe pieces. Then add a corner block to the ends of each row and press. Add these rows to the top and bottom of the quilt center.

FINISHING IT UP

Refer to The Finish Line on page 75 for details regarding each of these steps.

1. Layer the quilt top, batting, and backing; then baste, unless you plan to take your quilt to a longarm quilter.

2. Hand- or machine-quilt as desired. I machine-quilted the center of this quilt with a large sweeping paisley pattern and then used stylized stippling in the border areas. As I quilted, I avoided stitching through the half-circles as I wanted those to remain free.

3. After the quilting is finished, it's time to trim the outside border so the longer strips have an outside curve, the shorter strips have an inside curve, and the quilt corners are rounded. Refer to the quilt photograph for reference. Use the same circle template that you used to cut the circles for the inside border. Align the template as shown on page 46 and trace around it on each strip and at the corners. Use the center line for placement on the shorter strips. Then trim the quilt.

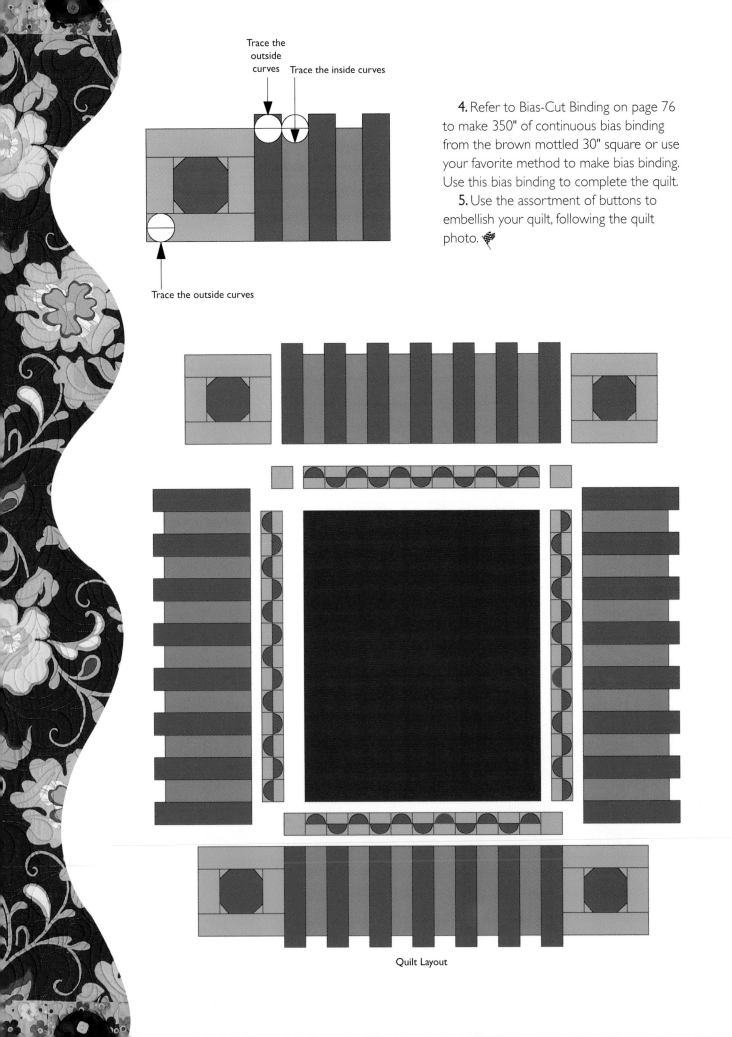

Trace the
outside
curves   Trace the inside curves

4. Refer to Bias-Cut Binding on page 76 to make 350" of continuous bias binding from the brown mottled 30" square or use your favorite method to make bias binding. Use this bias binding to complete the quilt.

5. Use the assortment of buttons to embellish your quilt, following the quilt photo.

Trace the outside curves

Quilt Layout

SUMMER HIGHWAY, 66" x 73", by Susan Nelsen

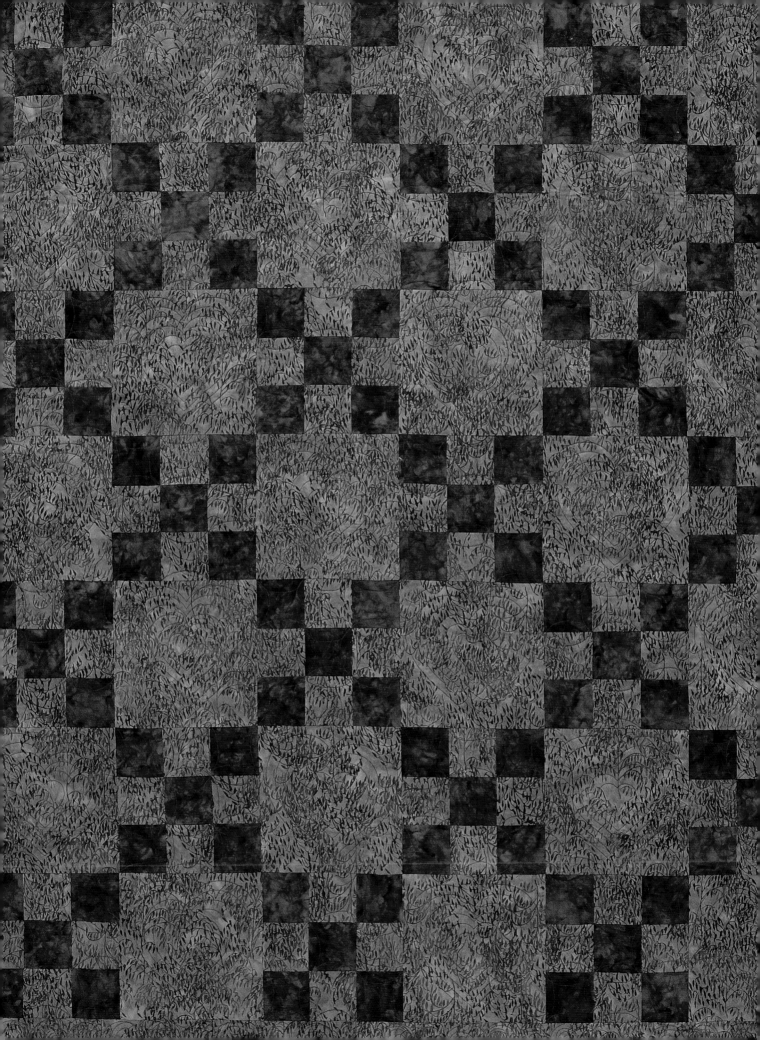

Country Curves

← **This Exit**

With our No-Fear approach to curves, it will be smooth driving ahead—even on foreign roads! The old favorite Irish Chain gets a new look with gently curved edges, rich shades of earthen brown and deep blue set off by sparkling jeweled embellishments. At the finish line we've added even more of a twist to the traditional with dimensional flowers and leaves.

Finished Quilt: 67" × 67"
Finished Block: 7½" × 7½"

What You'll need

All yardages are based on 42"-wide fabric.

✧ 2½ yards of brown mottled for the blocks, flowers, and bias binding

✧ 3¾ yards of teal print for the blocks, border, and flowers

✧ 75" × 75" piece of backing fabric

✧ 75" × 75" piece of batting

✧ 36" × 36" piece of batting for appliqué flowers

✧ Template plastic

✧ Freezer paper

✧ 16 buttons or jewels for the flower centers

CUTTING IT UP

— *All measurements include ¼"-wide seam allowances.*

— *Templates A, B and C for this project are on page 80. Copy the templates at 100% and trace onto template plastic. Cut out the templates.*

From the brown mottled, cut:

✧ 10 strips 3" × 42"

✧ 1 square 28" × 28" (for binding)

From the teal print, cut:

✧ 5 strips 8" × 42"; cut into 24 squares 8" × 8"

✧ 6 strips 7½" × 42"

✧ 8 strips 3" × 42"

Cutting and Making the Dimensional Flowers

1. To cut the flower and leaf shapes, place 2 pieces of the appropriate fabric, right sides together on top of a piece of batting. Using the templates, draw around the appropriate pattern pieces and cut through all of the layers. Pin the layers of each shape together so that they remain intact once they are cut. Repeat to cut the required number of layered pieces as follows:

    16 brown flowers, using pattern A

    32 brown leaves, using pattern C

    16 blue flowers, using pattern B

2. With the batting side down, sew around each flower and leaf shape using a ¼" seam allowance. Clip the seams of the flower shapes as shown and trim the points of the leaf shapes. Cut a 1"-long slit through the center of the top layer of fabric and turn the shapes right side out; press. Set these aside until later.

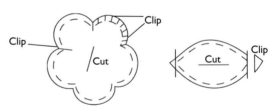

Making the Nine-Patch Blocks

1. Sew a teal 3" × 42" strip between 2 brown 3" × 42" strips as shown. Press the seam allowances toward the brown. Make 4 strip sets. Then cut fifty 3" units.

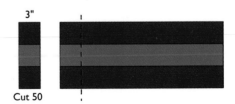

2. Sew a brown 3" × 42" strip between 2 teal 3" × 42" strips as shown. Press seam allowances toward the brown. Make 2 strip sets. Then cut twenty-five 3" units.

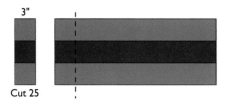

3"

Cut 25

3. Join a unit from step 2 between 2 units from step 1 as shown to complete one block. Press the seam allowances away from the center row. Repeat to make a total of 25 blocks.

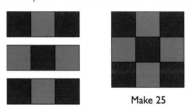

Make 25

PUTTING IT TOGETHER

1. Arrange the blocks and the teal 8" squares into seven horizontal rows as shown, alternating the position of the blocks and the squares in each row and from row to row as shown. Sew the blocks in each row together, pressing the seam allowances toward the teal squares. Join the rows. Press the seam allowances in one direction.

2. Refer to Borders on page 75 and use the teal print 7½" strips for the border.

Quilt Layout

Curves Ahead!

FINISHING IT UP

Refer to The Finish Line on page 75 for details regarding each of the following steps.

1. Layer the quilt top with the batting and the backing; then baste, unless you plan to take your quilt to a longarm quilter.

2. Hand- or machine-quilt as desired. I machine-quilted this quilt using a heart template in the center of each blue block. I used free-motion quilting to do a cathedral window motif in the Nine-Patch blocks and quilted freewheeling spirals on the border.

3. Refer to Round the Baseline on page XX to cut the scalloped edges along the border of your quilt.

4. Refer to Bias-Cut Binding on page 76 to make 285" of 2½"-wide continuous bias binding from the brown mottled 28" square or use your favorite method to make bias binding. Use this bias binding to complete the quilt.

5. Arrange the flower and leaf shapes on the quilt top as shown in the quilt photo. Secure them to the quilt by sewing through all layers along the quilting lines indicated on the patterns.

6. Attach jewels or buttons to the center of each flower.

7. Sew a hanging sleeve to the back of the quilt if desired.

COUNTRY CURVES, 67" × 67", by Loraine Manwaring

Shamrock Square

A SECOND CURVE OF COLOR

The curves are the same, but the look is different in this classic emerald green and white version of Irish Curves. Unforgettable travel to Ireland, the city of Dublin, and the beautiful Wicklow Mountains inspired this traditional favorite. Small green buttons and appliquéd shamrocks add touches of elegance.

SHAMROCK SQUARE, 67" x 67", by Loraine Manwaring

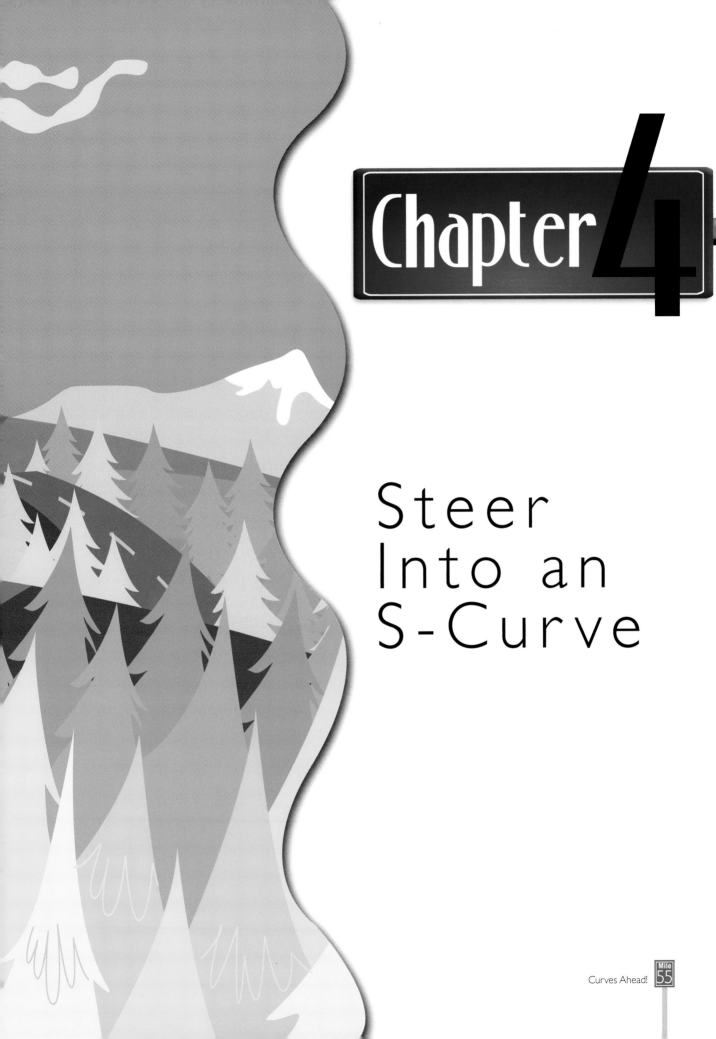

Chapter 4

Steer Into an S-Curve

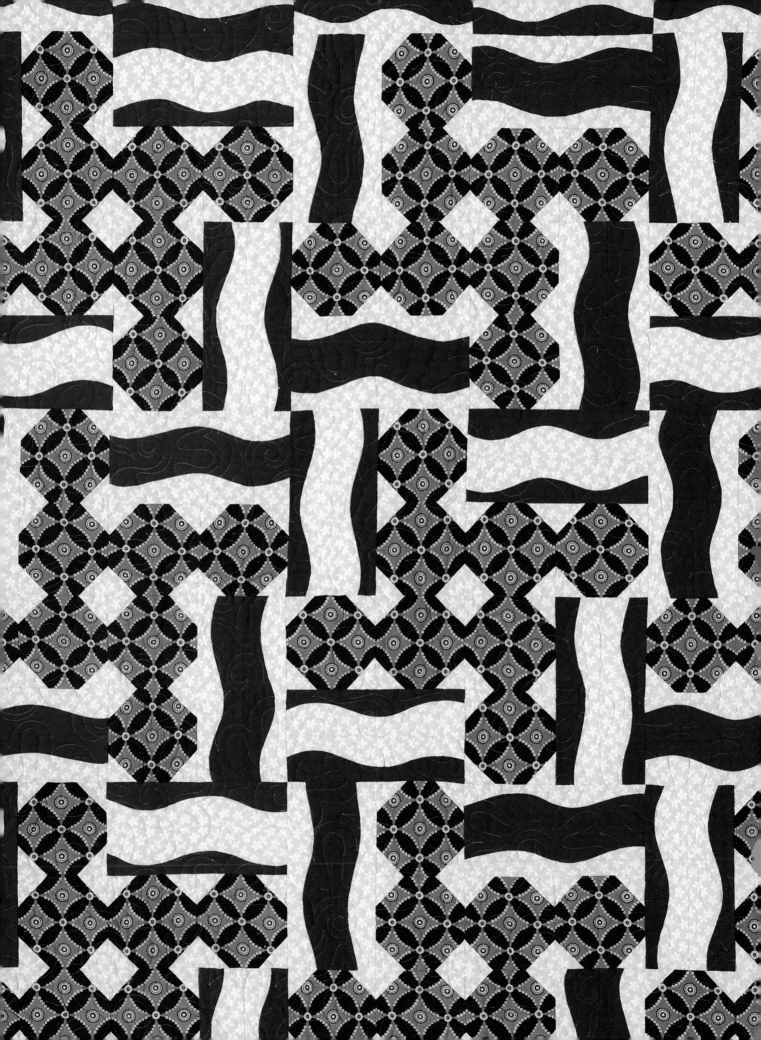

Moroccan Motorway

← **This Exit**

Dramatic curves everywhere ... but relax! With our Steer Into an S-Curve technique, you'll handle them easily. Just three fabrics—a bold print and two complementary small prints—create this exotic-looking curvy quilt. It will pop with contrast as you use bold fabrics to face the curves head on!

Finished Quilt: 62" × 80"
Finished Block: 9" × 9"

What You'll Need

All yardages are based on 42"-wide fabric.

✧ 3 yards of blue print for the blocks and border*

✧ 3 yards of yellow-green print for the blocks

✧ 2¼ yards of dark blue tone-on-tone for the blocks and binding

✧ 70" × 88" piece of backing fabric

✧ 70" × 88" piece of batting

✧ 1"-wide blue painter's tape

*Additional fabric will be needed if you fussy cut the blocks and border like I did.

CUTTING IT UP
– All measurements include ¼"-wide seam allowances.

From the blue print, cut:
✧ 12 strips 5" × 42"; cut into 96 squares 5" × 5"
✧ 7 strips 4" × 42"

From the yellow-green print, cut:
✧ 19 strips 2" × 42"; cut into 384 squares 2" × 2"
✧ 12 strips 4" × 42"; cut into 24 strips 4" × 21"

From the dark blue tone-on-tone, cut:
✧ 12 strips 4" × 42"; cut into 24 strips 4" × 21"
✧ 8 strips 2½" × 42" (for binding)

MAKING THE BLOCKS
You'll make the Snowballs and the curved Rails, and then combine them into the A and B blocks for the quilt top.

Snowballs
1. Using a soft-lead pencil and a see-through ruler, draw a diagonal line from corner to corner on the back of each green 2" square.

2. With right sides together, place a green 2" square on each corner of a blue 5" square as shown. Stitch on the drawn lines. Trim the seams to ¼" and press the triangles toward the corners. Repeat to complete 96 Snowballs.

Make 96

3. Sew the Snowballs into pairs as shown and press. Set these sections aside for now.

Make 48

Curved Rails
1. Refer to Steer Into an S-Curve on page 8, Single S-Curve. Use the green and dark blue 4" × 21" strips to make 11 sections with a blue center curve and 13 sections with a green center curve. Trim each section to 5" wide.

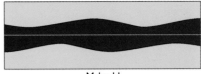

Make 11

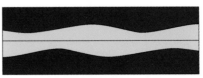

Make 13

2. From the blue center curve sections, cut 22 units 5" × 9½". From the green center curve sections, cut 26 units 5" × 9½".

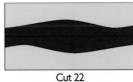

Cut 22

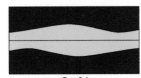

Cut 26

A and B Blocks

1. To make block A, sew a Snowball section to a blue center curve section as shown and press. Repeat to complete a total of 22 A blocks.

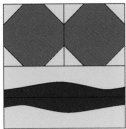

Block A Make 22

2. To make block B, sew a Snowball section to a green center curve section as shown and press. Repeat to complete a total of 26 B blocks.

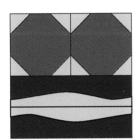

Block B Make 26

PUTTING IT TOGETHER

1. Refer to the quilt layout and alternate 3 A and 3 B blocks to make the top and bottom rows. Sew these blocks into rows.

2. Arrange 4 A blocks together, turning the blocks as shown. Join these into 1 unit. Repeat to make a total of 4 units.

3. Arrange 4 B blocks together, turning the blocks as shown. Join these into 1 unit. Repeat to make a total of 5 units.

4. Sew the A and B units into rows as shown. Join the rows together.

5. Referring to Borders on page 75, use the blue print 4" strips for the outside border.

FINISHING IT UP

Refer to The Finish Line on page 76 for details regarding each of these steps.

1. Layer the quilt top, batting, and backing; then baste, unless you plan to take your quilt to a long-arm quilter.

2. Hand- or machine-quilt as desired. Because this quilt is already so striking, I used a cream-colored thread and an overall pattern of swirls and flowers.

3. Use the dark blue tone-on-tone 2½" strips to bind the edges of the quilt.

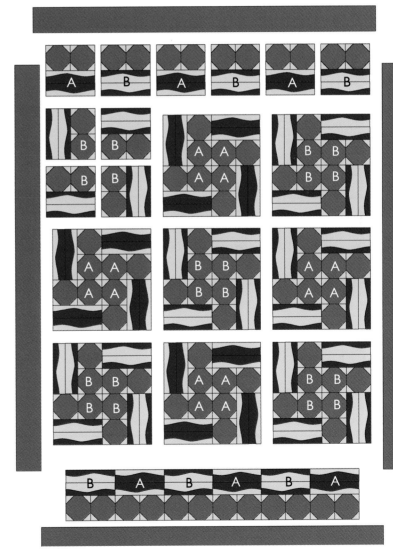

Quilt Layout

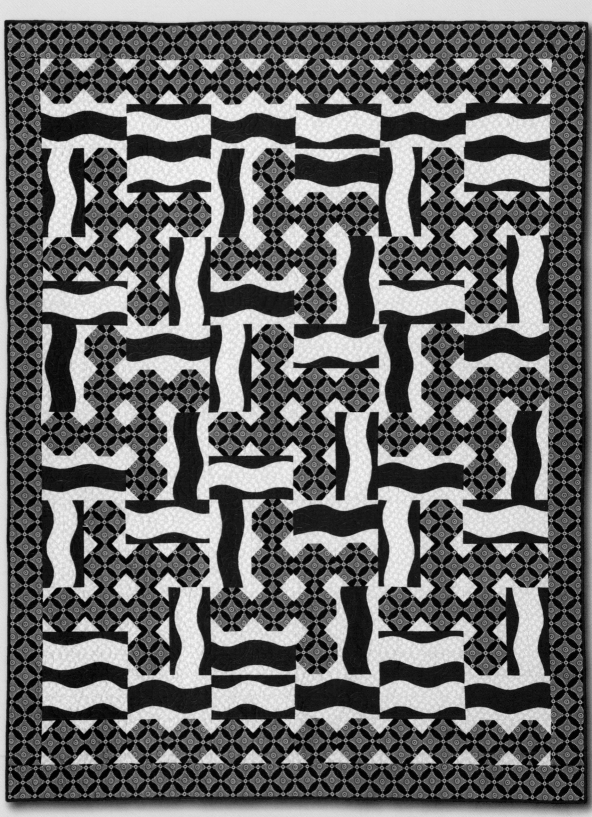

MOROCCAN MOTORWAY, 62" x 80", by Susan Nelsen

Red Light, Green Light

SECOND CURVE OF COLOR

Stop and go along the highway of your quilting road trip with No-Fear of the Curves Ahead. This exciting version of Moroccan Motorway combines the perfect mix of colors, patterns, and curves to create a wildly different look. The striped, mitered border is just the right touch at the finish line. This is Susan's favorite of all the curvy quilts she made for this book.

RED LIGHT, GREEN LIGHT, 66" x 84", by Susan Nelsen

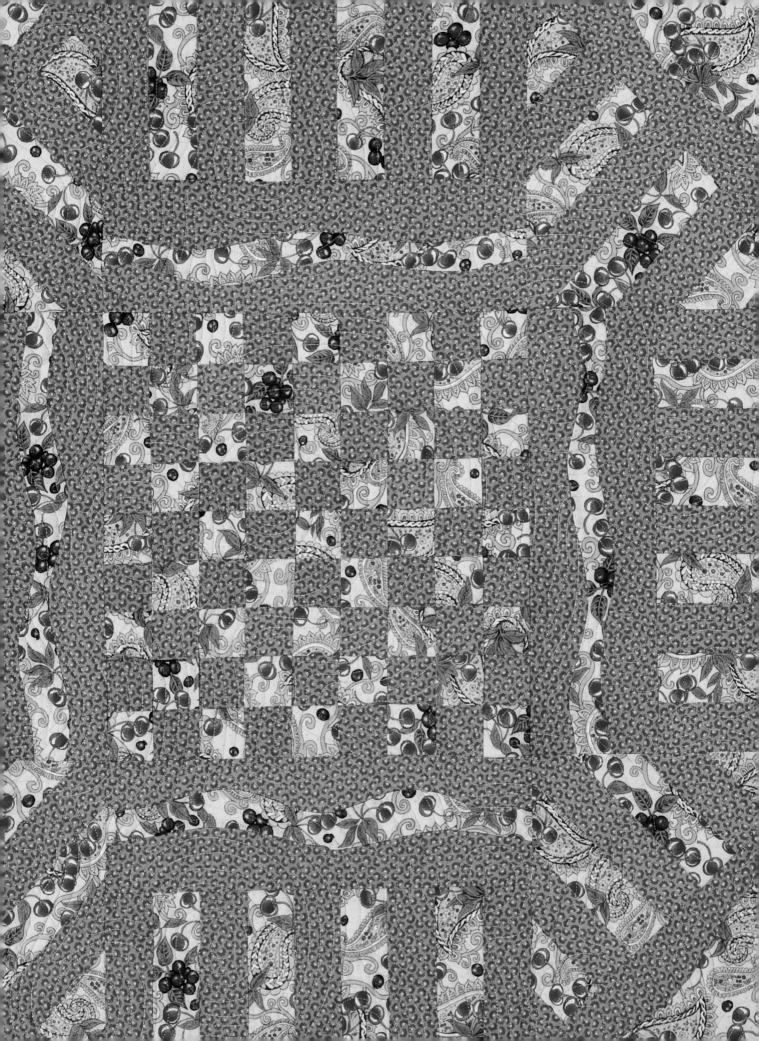

Mulberry Street

← **This Exit**

Life is easy, and so are the curves, as you travel along Mulberry Street. You'll find gentle curves around every corner, but with our Steer Into an S-Curve technique you'll be relaxed and ready to navigate them. Create this charming quilt for the center of the table using only two fabulous fabrics to create the fun, freehand curves.

Finished Quilt: 47" × 47"
Finished Block: 13½" × 13½"

What You'll Need

All yardages are based on 42"-wide fabric.

✧ 2½ yards of yellow floral for the background

✧ 2 yards of pink print for the doily and bias binding

✧ 53" × 53" piece of backing fabric

✧ 53" × 53" piece of batting

✧ Freezer paper, 12" × 12"

✧ 1"-wide blue painter's tape

CUTTING IT UP

– *All measurements include ¼"-wide seam allowances.*

From the yellow floral, cut:

✧ 2 strips 14½" × 42"; cut into 4 squares 14½" × 14½"

✧ 5 strips 3½" × 42"

✧ 4 strips 2½" × 42"; cut into 8 pieces 2½" × 15"

✧ 3 strips 2" × 42"; cut into 16 pieces 2" × 7"

✧ 6 strips 2" × 42"

From the pink print, cut:

✧ 4 strips 3" × 42"; cut into 8 pieces 3" × 15"

✧ 4 strips 2½" × 42"; cut into 4 pieces 2½" × 20" and 4 pieces 2½" × 15"

✧ 4 strips 2" × 42"; cut into 20 pieces 2" × 7"

✧ 6 strips 2" × 42"

✧ 1 square 22" × 22" (for binding curved outer edges) or 5 strips 2½" × 42" (for binding straight outer edges)

MAKING THE BLOCKS

You'll make 3 different blocks for this little quilt. Two of the blocks have freehand-cut curves, using the Steer Into an S-Curve technique on page XX.

Center Block

1. Sew a pink 2" × 42" strip between 2 yellow 2" × 42" strips and press the seam allowances toward the pink strip. Then cut fourteen 2" sections as shown. Call these A sections.

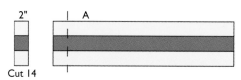

Cut 14

2. Sew a yellow 2" × 42" strip between 2 pink 2" × 42" strips and press the seam allowances toward the pink strips. Then cut thirteen 2" sections as shown. Call these B sections.

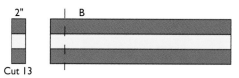

Cut 13

3. Alternate 5 A sections with 4 B sections and sew together as shown. Press the seam allowances in the same direction. Make 2 rows.

 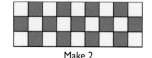

Make 2

4. Alternate 5 B sections with 4 A sections and sew together as shown. Press the seam allowances in the same direction.

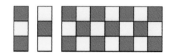 

Make 1

5. Sew the row from step 4 between the 2 rows from step 3 and press.

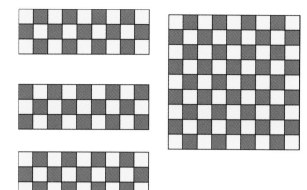

Corner Blocks

1. Cut a 12" × 12" freezer-paper template, and set aside for right now.

2. Cut the remaining 2" × 42" pink and yellow strips into pieces as needed and sew together to cover the template diagonally as shown. (Use the freezer-paper as a guide only at this point. Do not press it onto the stitched unit.)

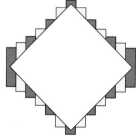

3. Press all the seams toward the pink strips. Center and press the freezer-paper template to the stitched unit. With your rotary cutter and ruler, trim around the freezer-paper square as shown. Remove the freezer paper. Repeat to make a second identical square, using the same freezer-paper template. Handle the completed squares carefully; the edges are bias and will stretch easily.

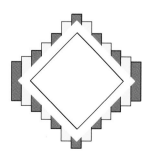

Make 2

4. Cut both squares diagonally corner to corner as shown to make 4 triangles and set these aside for now.

Cut 4 triangles

5. Cut a triangle off each yellow 14½" square as shown. Make each leg of the triangle 12". Discard these triangles.

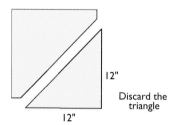

12"

Discard the triangle

12"

6. Refer to Steer Into an S-Curve, Single S-Curve on page 7 and follow the instructions to join a pink 2½" × 20" piece to the remaining section of the square with a curved seam. Trim the short ends of the pink strip even with the yellow square and trim the long edge of the pink strip so that it is straight. Repeat to make 4.

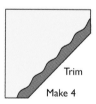

Trim

Make 4

7. Sew a pieced triangle from step 4 to the unit from step 6 and square up the block to 14" × 14". Repeat to make a total of 4 corner blocks.

Make 4

Outside Center Blocks

1. Alternate 5 pink 2" x 7" pieces with 4 yellow 2" x 7" pieces and sew together. Press the seams toward the pink strips. Make 4.

Make 4

2. Refer to Steer Into an S-Curve, Double S-Curve on page 9 and join a yellow 2½" x 15" piece to a pink 2½" x 15" piece. With the curved seam approximately centered in the length of the section, trim the section to 3½" x 14". Repeat to make 4 sections.

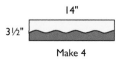

14"

3½"

Make 4

3. Using the same technique for the curved seams, join a yellow 2½" x 15" piece to a pink 3" x 15" piece. Then add another pink 3" x 15" piece against the yellow strip. With the yellow strip approximately centered in the length of the section, trim the section to 4½" x 14". Repeat to complete 4 sections.

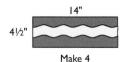

14"

4½"

Make 4

4. To make one block, sew a section from step 1 between one section from step 2 and one from step 3 as shown. Complete 4 blocks.

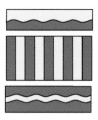
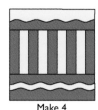

Make 4

PUTTING IT TOGETHER

1. Arrange the blocks as shown in the quilt layout. Sew the blocks into rows and then join the rows. Don't worry that all the pink seams don't line up exactly. Remember that these curves are cut freehand and that's the charm of this project. Look at the quilt photo to see the lacy edges of my doily—my seams don't all line up perfectly.

2. Refer to Borders on page 75 and use the yellow 3½" strips for the outside border.

FINISHING IT UP

Refer to The Finish Line on page 75 for details regarding each of these steps.

1. Layer the quilt top, batting, and backing; then baste, unless you plan to take your quilt to a longarm quilter.

2. Hand- or machine-quilt as desired. Because this quilt is quite busy already, I used an over-all quilting design with cream-colored thread to add texture to the quilt.

3. To cut the curved outside edges, refer to Fast S-Curve Finish on page 11. If you prefer, you may leave outside edges straight and bind them with straight-cut binding.

4. Refer to Bias-Cut Binding on page 76 to make 165" of continuous bias binding from the pink print 22" square or use your favorite method to make bias binding. Use this bias binding to complete the quilt. 🌿

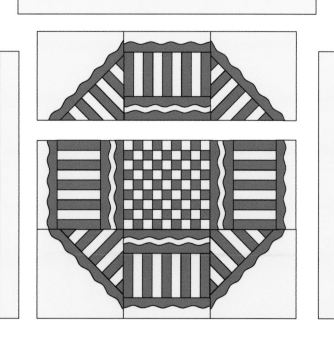

Quilt Layout

MULBERRY STREET, 47" x 47", by Susan Nelsen

Windmill Way

← **This Exit**

Imagine your quilting road trip has taken you to the tulip fields of Holland. Don't worry about the curves ahead. With our Tame a C-Curve technique, you'll have them all under control. Windmills whirring in the background combine with finishing touches of rick rack and vintage buttons to create this fanciful curvy quilt.

Finished Quilt: 41" × 56"
Finished Block: 5" × 5"

What You'll Need

All yardages are based on 42"-wide fabric.

✧ 1¾ yards of cream print for the background
✧ 1 yard of black floral for the border and binding
✧ ½ yard of green print for the windmills
✧ ½ yard of light green plaid for the windmill blades
✧ ½ yard of yellow dot for the center flower and inside border
✧ ½ yard of red dot for the flowers
✧ 49" × 64" piece of backing fabric
✧ 49" × 64" piece of batting
✧ 11½ yards of red jumbo rick rack
✧ 3½ yards of yellow jumbo rick rack
✧ Template plastic
✧ Water-soluble marker
✧ 5 yards of ¼" double-sided transparent, water-soluble tape
✧ 5 buttons, 2"-diameter
✧ Monofilament thread
✧ 1"-wide blue painter's tape

CUTTING IT UP

− All measurements include ¼"-wide seam allowances.

− Templates A and B for this project are on page 78. Copy the templates at 100% and trace onto template plastic. Cut out the templates and mark the dots as indicated on each template. Cut the B pieces as shown.

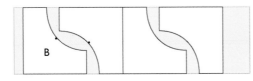

From the cream print, cut:

✧ 2 strips 8⅜" × 42"; cut into 5 squares 8⅜" × 8⅜", cut diagonally twice for a total of 20 setting triangles (discard 2)
✧ 2 squares 4½" × 4½", cut diagonally once for a total of 4 corner triangles
✧ 3 strips 5½" × 42"; cut into 10 squares 5½" × 5½" and and 16 pieces 3" × 5½"
✧ 2 strips 5½" × 42"; cut into 20 pieces, using template B
✧ 1 strip 2" × 42"; cut into: 16 squares 2" × 2"
✧ 2 strips 1½" × 42"

From the black floral, cut:

✧ 1 strip 14" × 42"
✧ 6 strips 2½" × 42" (for binding)

From the yellow dot, cut:

✧ 1 strip 6½" × 42"
✧ 1 strip 4¼" × 42"; cut into 4 pieces, using template A

From the red dot, cut:

✧ 2 strips 4¼" × 42"; cut into:16 pieces, using template A

From the green print, cut:

✧ 1 strip 5½" × 42"; cut into 4 squares 5½" × 5½"
✧ 3 strips 3" × 42"; cut into 6 strips 3" × 21"

From the light green plaid, cut:
✧ 3 strips 3" × 42"; cut into 6 strips 3" × 21"

MAKING THE BLOCKS
You'll make Drunkard's Path blocks for the flowers and blocks with freehand curves for the blades of the windmills.

Drunkard's Path Blocks
1. Refer to Tame a C-Curve on page 7 and follow the instructions to make 20 blocks, using all the red and yellow A pieces and the cream B pieces to make the color combinations as shown.

Make 16   Make 4

2. Now is the time to apply the contrasting rick rack to the curves of these blocks, using yellow rick rack on the red blocks and red rick rack on the yellow blocks. I used monofilament thread as the top thread with a small zigzag stitch to secure the trim.

Windmill Blade Blocks
1. Refer to Steer Into an S-Curve, Single S-Curve on page 8 and join each light green 3" × 21" strip to a green 3" × 21" strip with a curved seam. Square up the ends of each section. With the curved seam approximately centered in the length of the section, trim the section to 3" wide.

2. From the green strip sets, cut 16 sections 3" × 5½".

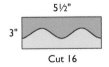 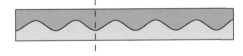

5½"

3"

Cut 16

3. Draw a diagonal line from corner to corner on the back of each cream 2" square, using a see-through ruler and a soft-lead pencil.

4. Position a cream square on one light green corner of a section from step 2 as

shown. Stitch on the drawn line. Trim the seam to ¼" and press toward the corner. Repeat this to complete 16 sections. Be consistent so that the triangle is on the same light green corner of each section.

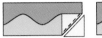

Make 16

5. Use the sections from step 4 and the cream 3" × 5½" pieces to make 16 blocks as shown.

Make 16

MAKING THE BORDER
1. Refer to Steer Into an S-Curve, Double S-Curve on page 7 and follow steps 1 through 7 to make the curved seam border section, using the black 14" × 42" strip and the yellow 6½" × 42" strip. This will make both the top and bottom sections. Trim both sections to 9½" × the maximum length possible with the ends squared up.

2. Add a cream 1½" strip to each border section as shown and press. Square up the ends of the sections and measure to see how long the borders sections are. Mine turned out to be 40½". Make sure that whatever length you have, both borders should be the same.

PUTTING IT TOGETHER
1. To make the quilt center, arrange the blocks, the cream 5½" squares, the setting triangles, and the corner squares as shown in the quilt layout.

2. Join the blocks into rows and then sew the rows together, adding the corner triangles last. Press this center section well.

3. Now don't get nervous, but depending on how long your border sections are, you may need to trim the sides of your quilt center to fit the top and bottom borders. Make sure that your quilt center is positioned with the cream blocks on the sides of the quilt as shown in the quilt layout. Measure through the horizontal center of your quilt. If this measurement is more than your border measurement, then trim the sides of the quilt center accordingly before adding the top and bottom borders. Refer to Borders on page 75 for more information.

FINISHING IT UP

Refer to The Finish Line on page 75 for details regarding each of these steps.

I. Layer the quilt top, batting, and backing; then baste, unless you plan to take your quilt to a longarm quilter.

2. Hand- or machine-quilt as desired. I added the red rick rack on top of the seam between the yellow and black borders as I machine quilted. I used monofilament thread as the top thread and a small zig zag stitch. The rest of the quilt is machine quilted with cream-colored thread, adding petals to the flowers, circles in the windmills, and a stylized stipple to the background.

3. Use the 2½" black floral strips to bind the quilt. As I sewed on the binding, I inserted the red jumbo rick rack in the seam so that half of the rick rack shows on the front of the quilt. This adds an interesting extra detail to the quilt.

4. Last of all, I added my five antique buttons as the flower centers.

Tip
I purchased these unique old buttons from Dusty's Vintage Textiles & Buttons of Holland, Massachusetts. I had no idea when or where I would use them (I do that all the time!). These buttons were probably used on a gentleman's coat in the 1890s and are made from the first plastic known, celluloid. I think they add the perfect charm to this project.—Susan

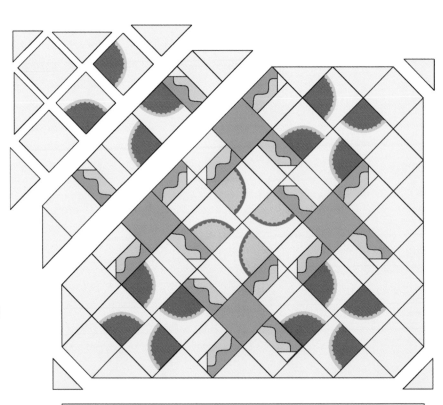

Quilt Layout

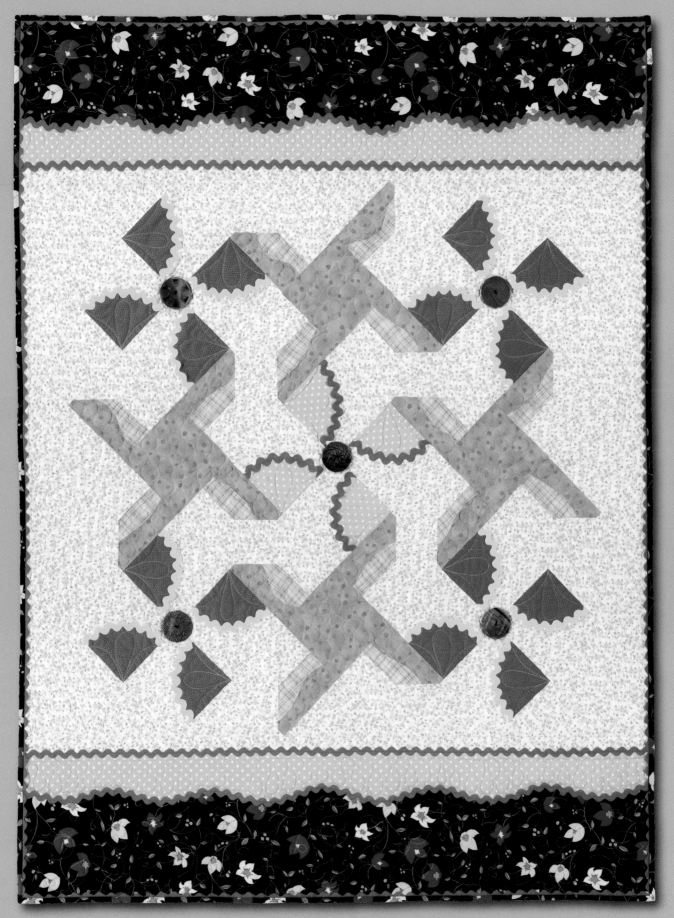

WINDMILL WAY, 41" x 56", by Susan Nelsen

Chapter 5

The Finish Line:
Quilting Basics to Take You to the Finish

These quilting basics will take to you to the final quilt finish. We share basic information to complete the projects in this book. However, you may use other methods that you prefer, and that's fine. Always practice accurate cutting, consistent ¼" seams, and careful pressing to get the most pleasing results. We hope you will relax and enjoy the whole quilting process!

BORDERS

Ideally, the best and flattest borders are cut from the lengthwise grain of the fabric rather than the crosswise grain, but to reduce fabric requirements, the patterns in this book use borders cut across the grain. If you prefer lengthwise borders, adjust the yardages accordingly.

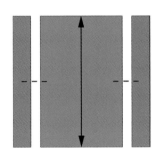

1. Measure the quilt through the vertical center, and cut two border strips to this measurement, joining strips as necessary. Mark the centers of the quilt edges and the border strips. Pin the border strips to the quilt sides, matching the center marks and ends, easing as necessary. Sew the border strips to the quilt and press seams toward the outside edges.

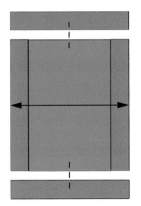

2. Measure your quilt through the horizontal center and cut two border strips to this measurement, piecing as necessary. Again mark the centers of the quilt edges and the border strips. Pin the border strips to the top and bottom edges of the quilt, matching the center marks and ends, easing as necessary. Sew the border strips to the quilt and press seams toward the outside edges.

PREPARING THE BACKING

Backing for your quilt should be 4" to 8" larger than the quilt top. If you will be using a longarm quilter, check with her about the required excess. It may be necessary to piece the backing with two or three lengths. Trim away the selvage edges and use a ½" seam allowance to sew the strips together. Press the seams open to reduce bulk.

LAYERING AND QUILTING

If you're taking your quilt to a longarm quilter, skip the following steps.

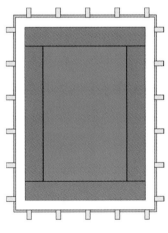

1. Spread the pressed backing on a flat, clean surface, wrong side up. Secure the edges with masking tape or pins. Smooth the batting over the backing so there are no wrinkles.

2. Center the pressed quilt top right side up on the batting, keeping the quilt edges parallel to the backing edges. Smooth the top and all the layers so there are no wrinkles.

3. Baste the layers together with hand stitching or use #1 nickel-plated safety pins placed 3" to 4" apart.

4. Hand- or machine-quilt using a pattern of choice. If this is your first try, check for books and stencils at your quilt shop to get you started.

BINDINGS—STRAIGHT AND BIAS

We use straight-cut binding for all quilts with straight outer edges and bias binding for quilts with curved outer edges. Trim the backing and batting even with the edges of your quilt top before adding the binding.

STRAIGHT-CUT BINDING

1. Join the strips with right sides together, using diagonal seams. Trim the seams to ¼" and press the seams open.

2. Trim one end of the long binding strip at a 45° angle. Turn the raw edge under ¼" and press. This will be your starting end. Press the strip in half lengthwise with wrong sides together.

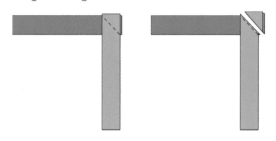

BIAS-CUT BINDING

> **TIP**
> Here's the formula for determining the size of the fabric square needed for this method of cutting bias binding:
> *Length of binding needed × width of binding = area of fabric*
> $$\sqrt{area\ of\ fabric} = \text{SIZE OF SQUARE}$$

1. Cut the appropriate size square of fabric in half diagonally as shown to make 2 triangles, then sew the 2 triangles, right sides together, with a ¼" seam allowance as shown. Press the seam open.

2. Use a straight edge to mark lines 2½" apart on the wrong side of the fabric as shown.

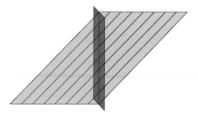

3. Make a tube by bringing the right sides together, off-setting the ends to make the lines match each other exactly. Sew the ends together with a ¼" seam allowance. Press the seam open.

4. Cut along the marked line to create the length of continuous bias binding. Turn the raw edge under ¼" on one end of the strip and press. This will be your starting end. Press the strip in half lengthwise with wrong sides together.

ADDING THE BINDING

1. Pick a beginning point on your quilt sandwich edge, away from a corner. Align the raw edges of the binding with the raw edges of the quilt, leaving about 3" tail of binding before beginning to stitch. Use a walking foot to stitch through all the layers, using a ¼" seam. Stop stitching ¼" from the corner, backstitch, and remove the quilt from under the needle.

2. Next, fold the binding straight up, forming a 45° angle. Then bring the binding straight down, aligning the edge of the binding with the edge of the quilt and the newly formed fold of binding even with the top edge of the quilt. Start stitching at the top edge and sew through all the layers using a ¼" seam, again stopping ¼" from the next corner. Repeat the process at each corner to continue around the quilt.

3. To join the binding when the ends meet, trim the finishing end to tuck neatly inside the starting end of the binding, and continue sewing the binding to the quilt.

4. Fold the binding over the raw edges of the quilt to the back so that the fold of the binding covers the machine stitching and hand stitch in place. At each corner fold the mitered fold in the opposite direction from the fold on the quilt front. 🏁

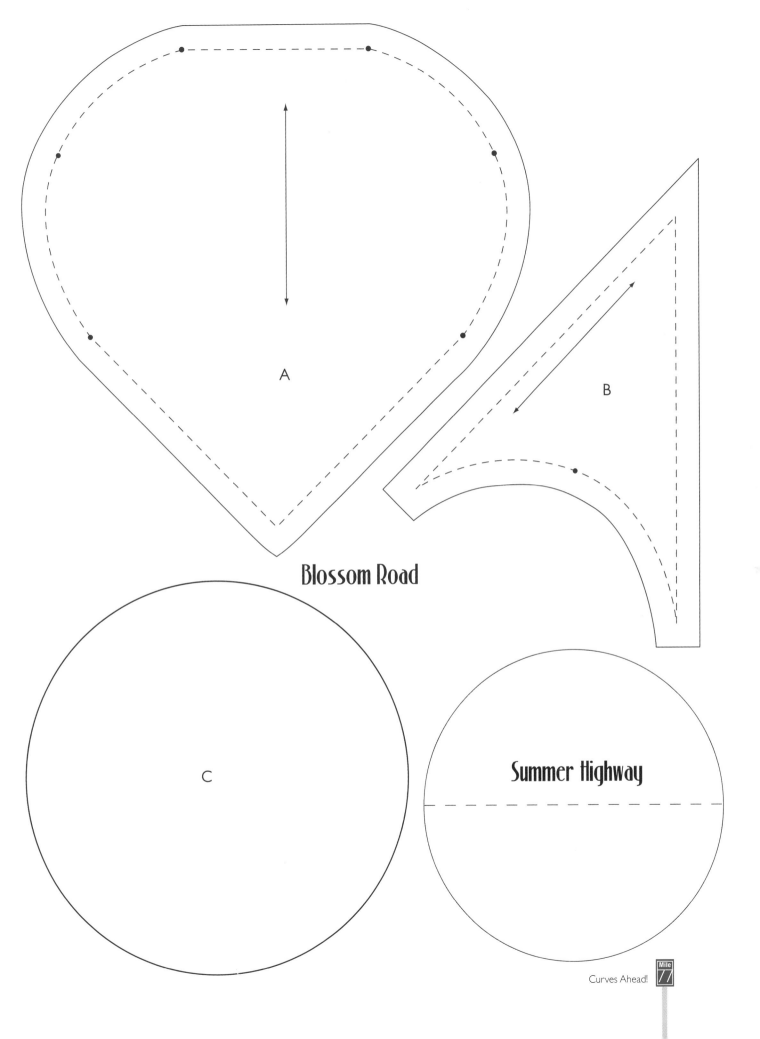

A

Blossom Road

B

C

Summer Highway

Curves Ahead!

Mile
77

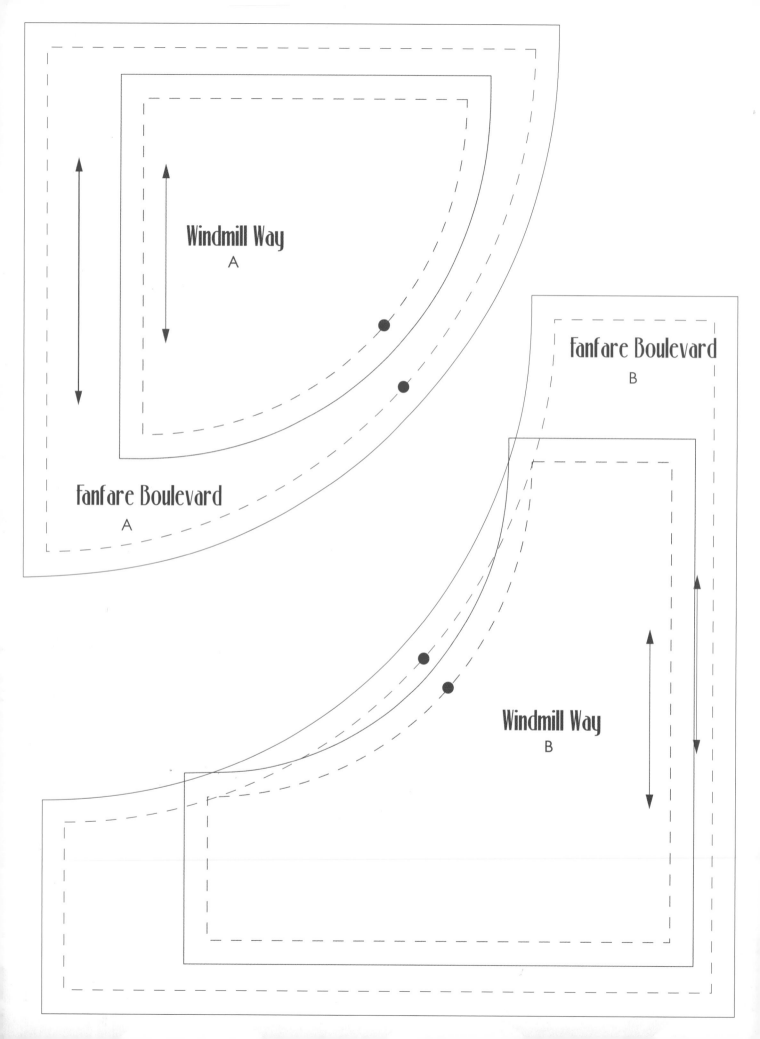

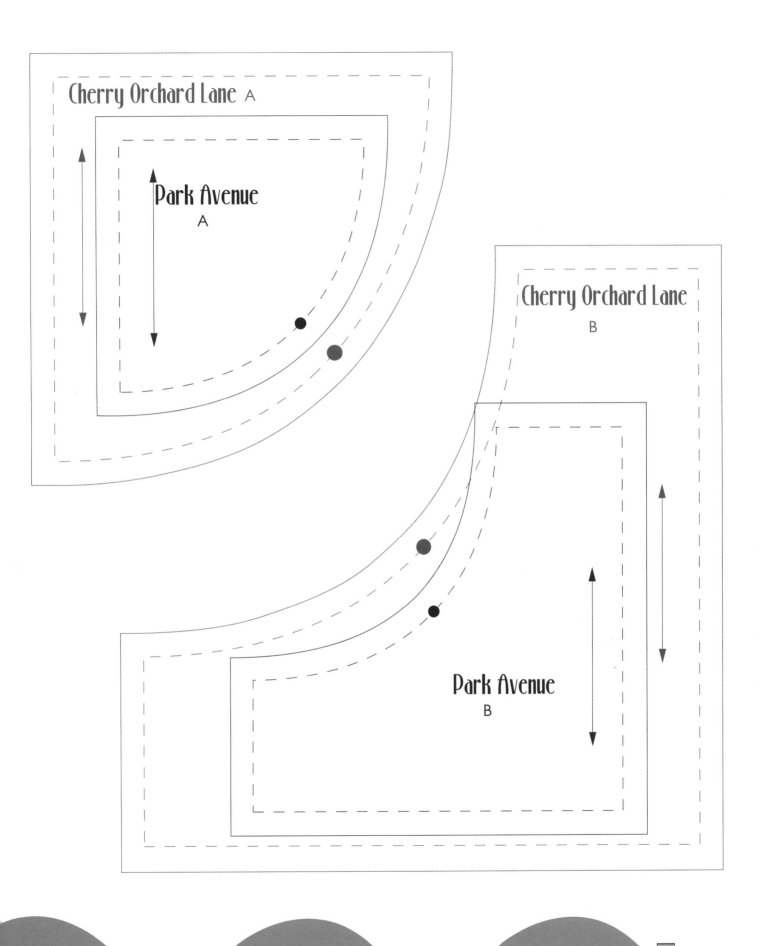

Cherry Orchard Lane A

Park Avenue
A

Cherry Orchard Lane
B

Park Avenue
B

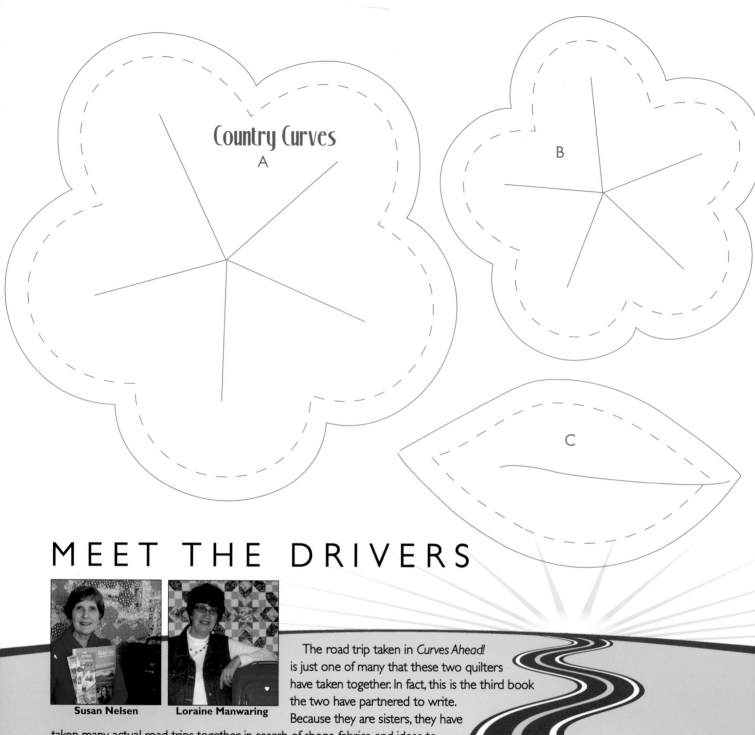

Country Curves

A

B

C

MEET THE DRIVERS

Susan Nelsen　　**Loraine Manwaring**

The road trip taken in *Curves Ahead!* is just one of many that these two quilters have taken together. In fact, this is the third book the two have partnered to write. Because they are sisters, they have taken many actual road trips together in search of shops, fabrics, and ideas to support their love of quilting. Susan and Loraine have great memories of piling several of their young children in the car and setting off in search of all of the items that are of interest to quilters. Later, as grandmothers, they have been free to take trips across the world, to visit markets and quilting events in search of fabrics and ideas for their books and quilting patterns.

Loraine has taught a variety of fabric art classes, as well as, beginning quilting classes. She has designed her own quilt patterns for many years, and enjoys lecturing at various quilt guilds. She is a longarm machine quilter, and the author of three books. Her home in the woods of Troy, Idaho, is overflowing with quilts, never-ending quilting projects, and the busy activities of eight grandchildren, who are frequent visitors.

Susan lives in Idaho Falls, Idaho, with her husband, Ken. She has authored seven books and is a freelance technical editor in the quilt-book publishing world. She is the owner of Rasmatazz Designs, her quilt design and publishing company, as well as, being the involved grandmother of seven great kids. As an active longarm machine quilter, she quilts her own quilts and those of others as well.